AUSTRALIA
THE BIG COUNTRY

AUSTRALIA
THE BIG COUNTRY

COLOUR LIBRARY BOOKS

As I sit writing these words in Fremantle, Western Australia, the office workers are leaving the old colonial buildings in Phillimore Street to head home to enjoy the last of the day's sunshine. It has been another warm, balmy day in Western Australia, with the state's top temperature of 45 degrees – around 116 degrees in the old scale – being reached in the Pilbara iron town of Goldsworthy.

Along the Fremantle waterfront, the crews of the 12-metre yachts, sunburned, dishevelled and exhausted, are returning for another day's practice in preparation for the world fleet championships being sailed in the choppy waters of the Indian Ocean. At the Lombardo's restaurant complex, squeezed among the brightly-painted fishing boats at the water's edge, the early diners are looking at menus and choosing between local blue manna crabs or the dhufish. In the colourful gold town of Kalgoorlie, 600 kilometres from Perth, miners in shorts and heavy boots head for the Boulder Block Tavern to swill the red dust out of their throats with glasses of ice-cold Swan lager.

Across the country, 4,350 kilometres away in Sydney, a noisy, excited crowd is engrossed in a game of cricket. It is 8 pm in Sydney, and those not screaming encouragement at the Sydney Cricket Ground are moving into the city centre for the evening's entertainment, perhaps in the fascinating Rocks area, birthplace of the nation, or maybe at a smart restaurant overlooking the harbour. What has happened in Sydney today? The evening paper carries a story on severe summer storms which brought hail across a wide area of the city.

On the Gold Coast, in the south east corner of Queensland, the pace is quickening at the Conrad International Hotel and Jupiters Casino as casually-dressed gamblers chase fortunes on the blackjack tables. By now, the sun has set over Ayers Rock in the Northern Territory, the stockmen are pulling off their boots after another arduous day, bedtime stories are being read to the children of the outback, the travelling carnivals are luring remote communities with their bright lights, and the nighttime cover is being pulled over this incredible country.

Tomorrow, the great Australian adventure will begin all over again, but now it is time for the country to count its blessings. Ruggedly beautiful, romantic and mineral-rich. Untamed, unsullied and unlimited in its ability to surprise and stimulate. The gold diggers and the grape pickers, the business tycoons and the cray fishermen, the wheat farmers and the sheep-shearers, the dockside workers and the iron-ore miners, all are united in believing that they have been given a special place on this earth in which to pursue their dreams.

Australia is a large and complex land of 4.8 million square kilometres, supporting a population of 16 million, 70 per cent of whom live in the five mainland state capitals of Sydney, Melbourne, Brisbane, Perth and Adelaide. As a comparison, the United Kingdom has a population three and a half times as large, in an area amounting to only three per cent of Australia's land mass.

Lucky is the man, if he exists, who can say that he has seen all of Australia. Most of us merely peep behind the curtain here and there, and become more enchanted with each new discovery. Like the Europeans who came freely to Australia, or were transported there in convict ships some 200 years ago, the modern-day adventurer feels a compulsion to go on in search of the myriad, sometimes mystical, experiences which this ancient continent has to offer.

Australia can be the sight of Sydney Harbour Bridge and the Opera House in early morning from the bow of the Manly ferry. It can be the awesome isolation of a 40,000 hectare Queensland cattle station, where the nearest neighbour might be 400 kilometres away. It can be an abandoned gold town in the rust-coloured outback of Western Australia, where corroding machinery and long-discarded beer bottles evoke memories of the leathery old men who tried to dig dreams out of the dirt. It can be the spectacular Ayers Rock sunset, listening to Aboriginals' tales of their ancestors. It can be the sight of buffalo on the Marrakai Plains, Northern Territory, or crocodiles on the South Alligator River. It can be the little alpine village of Banjo Paterson's 'Man from Snowy River' country, breathing the pure, cool air 1,370 metres above sea level. The list goes on, and for every settler, every visitor, there is a special memory, a moment frozen in time, a personal experience to be locked away and cherished.

No-one should think they have been to Sydney or Melbourne or the Gold Coast and seen Australia. Not when they haven't cruised the Murray Riverina region in New South Wales, or slept under the stars at Waterfall Creek in Kakadu National Park, Arnhem Land, or experienced the wilderness of the Franklin River National Park in Tasmania.

Yet, as beautiful and beguiling as these places are, they are just sweeps of the brush on the extraordinary canvas that is Australia. It is a land of richness and breathtaking contrast. A land of wildflowers, like the kangaroo paw, bachelor's button, mountain eyebright and spider orchid. It is a land of birds, like the blue-winged kookaburra, Albert lyre bird, Major Mitchell cockatoo, Regent bower bird, dancing brolga and spangled drongo. It is a land of mammals and reptiles, like the saltwater crocodile, thorny devil, tiger snake, koala, camel, wild buffalo and kangaroo.

It is the land of the spectacular, like Katherine Gorge, a magnificent river canyon in inland Australia, and Ayers Rock, 500-600 million years old – a giant red gemstone rising 348 metres above the plain from an 8 kilometre circumference. It is a land of strange-sounding places: Humpty Doo, Coober Pedy, Smiggin Holes, Barrow Creek, the Bungle Bungles and Mudgeeraba. It is a land of legendary people, bushrangers like Ned Kelly, Mad Dan Morgan and Captain Moonlight, whose spirit, if not their lawlessness, lives on today in a population which has had to battle hard to establish its new frontiers.

Two hundred years after the arrival of the first settlers, the task today for its cosmopolitan population – immigrant Greeks, Turks, Slavs, British, Italians, Vietnamese and Dutch – is to take the baton and keep the country moving away from parochialism, and towards proud and purposeful unity.

WESTERN AUSTRALIA
Western Australia, the biggest of all the states, occupies a third of the continent's land mass, sprawling over more than 2.5 million square kilometres and several climate zones. If many people – and I am including Australians – find it hard to comprehend the vastness of the country, then they are equally staggered by the size of Western Australia. You can fly for three hours in a modern jet and still be over Western Australian soil; you can drive for days and still be inside the state's boundaries. Superimposed on a map of Western Europe, Western Australia would stretch north to south from Oslo to Madrid and east to west from Dublin to Milan. Or, to draw another comparison, it is three and a half times bigger than Texas. This is the scale of Western Australia. And yet little more

than 1.4 million people populate this enormous area, and just over a million of them live in the state capital, Perth.

The tyranny of distance has made Perth the most isolated capital in the world. Adelaide, its nearest big city neighbour, is 1,700 kilometres to the east on the other side of the vast emptiness of the Nullarbor Plain. To the west is the great expanse of the Indian Ocean. To the south, the Southern Ocean, next stop Antarctica. And to the north, several thousand kilometres away, Indonesia. Perth is as close to Singapore as it is to the eastern gateway of Sydney, where Australia's founding fathers stepped ashore to colonise New Holland.

While this isolation has inherent disadvantages, it has had its benefits, too. Western Australia's flora and fauna, hemmed in by the natural barriers of sea and desert, have evolved in an environment unaffected by outside influences. Thus, many of its 8,000 or so varieties of wildflowers are unique to the state, most of them to the southwest corner. They have been given exquisitely appropriate names: the long-stemmed green and red kangaroo paw (Western Australia's floral emblem); the delicate spider orchid; the appealing donkey orchid; the rare carnivorous Albany pitcher plant. There are many, many more and in spring they carpet the countryside in a riotous floral rainbow, a canvas that applauds Mother Nature's handiwork.

Then there are the forests of karri and jarrah – among the world's most durable hardwoods and again unique to this botanic wonderland. The karri is a tree of immense beauty, growing up to 90 metres high, with up to a seven-metre girth. In the lush underworld below the green canopy are many rare animals and birds. You might be lucky enough to catch a glimpse of the numbat, a member of the marsupial family. This shy and reclusive creature with its distinctive black and white stripes and long tail is nowadays confined to a couple of relatively small areas of forest.

Visiting this 'Garden of Western Australia' quickly destroys the popular overseas misconception that Australia is a barren, sunburnt land, a harsh and unforgiving environment covered in little more than spinifex. Here, in the southwest corner, is rolling countryside as green and lush as you will find in the English county of Cornwall. There are fast flowing streams where you can fly-fish for rainbow trout; tranquil valleys covered in ferns and shrouded in mist; fruit-laden orchards; rugged mountains providing panoramic views of fertile farming land.

Here, too, are vineyards producing premium quality wines which have won world acclaim; quaint forest towns at Pemberton and Manjimup; coastal resorts like Dunsborough, Yallingup and Denmark; spectacular, rugged granite cliffs presenting a rampart to the pounding Southern Ocean rollers, and secluded, white sandy beaches. These are just some of the striking images and not-to-be-forgotten experiences awaiting the visitor.

For a sharply contrasting image take a trip some 600 kilometres east of Perth to the gold mining town of Kalgoorlie. 'Kal', as it is affectionately known by the locals, was created in the heady, turn-of-the-century gold rush boom which injected new life into the colony. The population of Western Australia doubled every five years following Irishman Paddy Hannan's gold discovery in the early 1890s. There were 100-plus mines within the area, then measured as the richest square mile on earth. In the fevered Kalgoorlie of that time, before the pipeline from the coast was built, water cost $6 a gallon and French champagne 20 cents a bottle.

In the 1970s, when gold prices plummeted, Kalgoorlie's heartbeat slowed just as dramatically. But, with the resurgence of gold's value, the town's pulse quickened and, having learned hard economic lessons from the slump, it is again a prosperous and thriving community. Major new discoveries have been made, and previously uneconomical mines have been brought back into operation.

'Kal', with its wide streets and old-style hotels (it once boasted a hotel on every corner), today retains the romance and atmosphere of the early boom days. At the Hainault Tourist Mine you can actually see how gold was originally mined. There are displays of old and new mining techniques, as well as of gold-pouring. Well worth including in any visit to the goldfields is the nearby town of Coolgardie, which has been preserved as a monument to the good ol' days. Others, like Gwalia, Broad Arrow and Orra Banda, have become ghost towns.

Two-up, a traditional Australian form of gambling, is another of Kalgoorlie's big drawcards. Until recently illegal, two-up has been played in the bush outside the town for years. The police mostly turned a blind eye to the game (as they do to the town's four brothels), occasionally launching raids to keep up appearances. Despite being given legal status, in Kalgoorlie alone, the game is still played in the same tin-roofed venue eight kilometres from town. Today, too, women are allowed to participate.

In the tropical far north of Western Australia the countryside and scenery change yet again. This area has been described as the last frontier, a sparsely populated wilderness region which has still to be explored by many Australians, let alone by the wider world. Minerals, which have played such a crucial role in Western Australia's development, thrust the Kimberley region onto the international stage when the world's biggest deposits of diamonds were discovered there in 1981. This is a land of great physical beauty – table-top mountains, rugged gorges, towering waterfalls and stunning coastal scenery. Close to the Northern Territory border is a geological wonder which has been rediscovered in recent years. The Bungle Bungles are a haunting moonscape of soft sandstone weathered over millions of years to form dome-shaped, bee-hive mountains.

Man has also contributed to the physical grandeur of the area. The Ord River was dammed in the 1960s in a bold bid to provide irrigation water for pioneering farmers. The lake this created, Lake Argyle, holds nine times the water of Sydney Harbour. It has become a popular water playground for increasing numbers of tourists.

There is only a handful of towns in the remote Kimberley. Broome is the most flamboyant and fascinating. In the 1900s the town was the pearling capital of the world, and attracted a polyglot population – Malays, Chinese, Japanese, Indonesians, Filipinos and Europeans. Many of their descendants still live in Broome, though these days it is tourism which has become the major industry following the decline in demand for pearls.

Broome has a tropical, exotic atmosphere with many oriental landmarks to remind you of its colourful, multi-cultural heritage. Mangrove swamps and beautiful beaches enhance the town's charm and appeal, as do the extraordinary tides which leave vessels marooned like beached whales as the water recedes almost to the horizon.

Southwest of the Kimberley is the Pilbara, Western Australia's 'red heart', where men and machines mine mountains of iron ore in the Hamersley Range. The Hamersley Range is famous also for its magnificent gorges around the inland town of Wittenoom, once an asbestos mining centre. Here, over millions of years, rivers have sliced through the soft rock like a wire cheese cutter, leaving chasms of sheer rockface hundreds of feet deep.

Further south, in the neighbouring Gascoyne region, is

Exmouth, a renowned game fishing centre, where you can test your skills against marlin, Spanish mackerel and a host of other fighting varieties. Several hundred kilometres inland is Mount Augustus, the largest monolith in the world, twice the size of Ayer's Rock. Heading south again is Shark Bay, where a family of dolphins regularly comes into the beach to be hand-fed by excited tourists wading in the shallows.

South-bound again and we arrive in the Mid West, a region of fertile farmlands, historic mining towns, stunning coastal cliffs and river gorges, and the Houtman Abrolhos Islands, graveyard to many ships which foundered on the reefs as early as 1629. These same reefs today provide a rich harvest of rock lobster which titillate the palates of gourmets in Japan, Europe and North America.

Now we are back in Perth, surely one of the world's most visually beautiful modern cities, basking in an average of eight hours sunshine daily throughout the year. Perth is a sparkling jewel, its skyscraper towers shimmering in the waters of the majestic Swan River as it flows past the city doorstep to the port city of Fremantle. Perth is pollution free, with clear blue skies, refreshingly clean air, wide, tidy streets and a river which has not been tainted by industrial waste. It is a magnificent aquatic playground that is jealously protected by the locals, who go there to swim, water-ski, sail and fish.

It is not hard to see why the inhabitants are so proud of their flourishing, wealthy city. Modern five-star hotels, a casino, oceanside leisure complexes, art galleries, entertainment centres and a thriving commercial and retail heart are evidence of Perth's growing maturity as an international city. In terms of distance, Perth is isolated, but it is very much a city keeping pace with the outside world. International airlines and modern communications have seen to that.

It has been said that Perth is one of the world's best kept secrets, but the America's Cup, yachting's premier trophy, prised open the doors to reveal her blue-watered brilliance.

SOUTH AUSTRALIA
First a curious fact which always surprises me about South Australia. It is the driest state in a continent not noted for its rainfall. I have always found that hard to accept when strolling down King William Road and across the River Torrens towards the Adelaide Oval cricket ground. But, beyond the parks and gardens and the churches and well-ordered residential areas are vast expanses of unpopulated arid desert – an alien land which serves to highlight Adelaide's coastal greenery.

Adelaide is an oasis of culture, fine wine, food and fun – an understated city of subtle tones, beautiful churches, calm and conservatism. The days when its staidness was a bit of a joke among the brasher Australians of Sydney and Brisbane have disappeared as Adelaide has built on its best features to reach a point today where many of its attractions, including its new casino in the old railway station, are envied throughout the rest of the country.

The Festival Centre, overlooking the River Torrens, has managed to achieve the near-impossible and equal Sydney's wonder-of-the-world Opera House. The complex, whose final stage was opened by the Queen in 1977, combines a 2,000-seat concert hall, two smaller theatres, an outdoor amphitheatre and a huge plaza displaying the largest outdoor work of art in Australia – the dramatic sculptures of West German artist Otto Hajek.

If Otto's ambitious art is something of a shock when seen for the first time, you can always take yourself down to the riverbank, perhaps to hire a pedal boat while you work out what it all means. And if you're still not sure, then you could lose yourself watching the spider monkeys in Adelaide Zoo, or stroll along Hindley Street among the restaurants and slightly naughty night clubs, where the city tries to throw off its maiden-aunt image.

Adelaide is a stroller's city. You walk a bit, stop a while, munch a sandwich in the park, stretch out around the water, close your eyes and let the bustle of the Rundle Street shopping mall fade into the background. Relaxation comes quickly, and when you open your eyes again it might be time to peep behind Adelaide's green-sleeved city and look towards the hills where another, different world emerges among the pleasant, English-style countryside.

Mount Lofty, a gentle half-hour drive from the city, rises 700 metres and gives a splendid view over Adelaide, particularly at night from Windy Point. Up here, among the rainbow-coloured parrots, the air is freshly-scented with forest flowers and the lingering salt-water breezes of the ocean. Up here, too, tucked away in the folds of the hills, are the little European-style villages where Italian and German traditions flourish strongly, seemingly held in a time warp, oblivious to the 20th century bustle of the big city just down the road.

Further away, to the north-east of Adelaide, is the Barossa Valley, where much of Australia's wine is produced. There are now vineyards and wineries in every state and mainland territory of Australia – even in the Northern Territory around Alice Springs – but for consistency and quality it is hard to match the wines of South Australia and the Hunter Valley in New South Wales.

In the Barossa Valley and in the Clare Valley, in the McLaren Vale, south of Adelaide, and in the rich red 'terra rosa' volcanic soils of Coonawarra, wines of outstanding quality are produced, and are being acclaimed as such throughout the world. Along the Murray River, downstream from the South Australia-Victoria border, the Riverland area – which includes the towns of Renmark, Berri, once a sheep-station but now a centre for fruit juice and dried fruit production, Loxton, Waikerie and Morgan – produces around 38 per cent of Australia's grapes.

But it is the Barossa Valley, where more than 30 wineries are squeezed into an area some 40 km long and between five and eleven kilometres wide, which attracts the most interest. First settled in the 1840s by German immigrants driven out of Prussia and Silesia by religous persecution, the Barossa (originally spelled Barrosa – Hill of Roses) soon established itself as exceptional wine-growing country.

Today you almost expect to see the Rhine River flowing past, so strong is the German influence in the region. The food here is mettwurst and blutwurst and sauerbraten, the music is Bavarian brass and the vineyards themselves have names like Krondorf, Kaiser Stuhl and the more recently founded Wolf Blass. Bethany was the first German settlement in the valley, although Tanunda is, today, the most German of the valley towns and some of the early settlers' cottages remain in the Ziegenmarkt – Goat Square.

Further north beyond the Barossa, past the vineyards and the orchards, the spectacular Flinders Ranges give way to South Australia's arid heart – kilometre after kilometre of inhospitable, flat scrub country. It was here that the late Donald Campbell attempted a land speed record – on a lake. This was possible as, apart from the rare occasions when it is in flood and becomes a dangerous inland sea, Lake Eyre is a dry, salt-pan wilderness.

The South Australian outback includes much of the Simpson Desert, prohibited Aboriginal reserves, and the opal mining settlements of Coober Pedy and Andamooka, where residents live underground to get relief from the extreme temperatures.

Australia is a contrast of climates and colours and landscapes, and in South Australia the differences come into even sharper relief. Away from the rocky, red-hot interior, the state can offer Australia's greatest river, the Murray, as it flows its last 650 kilometres to the sea.

From Waikerie, gateway to the Riverland, the Murray winds its way through vineyards, orchards, wheatfields, market towns, picnic areas and eucalyptus trees before flowing into Lake Alexandrina and finally disappearing into the Southern Ocean near Goolwa.

South of Adelaide, as the hills extend towards the Fleurieu Peninsula, there is another facet of South Australia. Saw-tooth rocks, buffeted by the high waves of the Southern Ocean, little bays and hidden inlets, steep cliffs and surfing beaches provide a magnificent seascape. This is the coast where the whalers once plied their trade, and where smugglers brought their illicit cargoes ashore before moving the contraband to Adelaide. Inland, there is the productive wine-growing region of the Southern Vales, while out to sea is Kangaroo Island – named by Matthew Flinders but first charted by the French explorer Nicholas Baudin. Around 150km long and 30km wide, Kangaroo Island is the third biggest island in Australia and – although it is little more than 100km from Adelaide – its isolation has allowed natural, rugged beauty and native wildlife to survive unspoiled.

This, then, is South Australia: the festival city of Adelaide; the paddle-steamered splendour of the Murray and the grape-strung richness of the Barossa; the desert mountain beauty of the Flinders Ranges and the harsh expanses of the interior. A State of dramatic and dazzling variety.

NORTHERN TERRITORY

The Aboriginal races have lived in Australia for tens of thousands of years, driven to a strange new land from southeastern Asia to roam a harsh, eerie, unfamiliar desert landscape. There is nowhere in Australia where the Aboriginal spirit lives on as it does in the Northern Territory, a vast untamed region of giant monoliths, lost canyons, gorges, rare animals, dancing birds, contrasting colours and staggeringly-beautiful sunrises and sunsets.

The Northern Territory covers more than 1.3 million square kilometres and is five times as big as Britain, four times as big as Japan and twice the size of Texas. A quarter of its 143,000 population are Aboriginal and this is their land – the land of the Dreamtime.

Dreamtime is the time before time. The time even before the Dreaming, the Aboriginal's spiritual understanding of all that he knows, of all that has been passed on to him since birth.

This is the land of legends and myths, and to cross the Northern Territory from the Red Centre to the Top End, the tropical north, is to pass through time itself. It is a silent, mystical world of sacred caves containing ancient tribal art; of unexplored, burning desert; of meteorite craters and tropical glades, billabongs and lagoons. Man has been here for around 50,000 years, but the Red Centre remains majestically aloof, awesome in its power to swallow up the senses and store its secrets in the desert dust. Only nature has the capacity to change things here. Man can but come and look and learn and be humbled.

Here the Aboriginals tell their Dreamtime tales, of the old blind woman Mundungkala, who burst through the earth's surface bearing the tribes in her hands. In the darkness she created the dawn of man by scattering the figures across the flat earth. The wind, the rain, the stars, the birds and the animals provide the source of these myths, which helped to establish and preserve the nomadic Aboriginal way of life.

There is the legend of Tiddalik, the giant frog, who awoke one morning with a raging thirst and drank all the fresh water, turning the tropical green Centre into the arid heart of Australia. With the other animals in despair, the eel, Nabunum, began to dance and when Tiddalik laughed, water flowed out from his mouth to replenish the lakes and rivers.

Another legend explains how a girl who loved dancing was saved from the north wind by two spirits from the lake who transformed her into a brolga, a showy, long-legged bird whose remarkable courtship dance is still one of the wonders of outback Australia.

Today's dreamers come in the air-conditioned luxury of Australian Pacific coaches, or barrel along in Japanese four-wheel drives, or sway through the sand dunes on camels ($50 a day, unlimited mileage), absorbing some of the mysticism and spirit of the Never, Never Land. They follow in the footsteps of the great explorers like John McDougall Stuart, John Ross, Ernest Giles and the pastoralists, railway workers, telegraph line men and miners who fought their way across this harsh, unrelenting land. At Chambers Pillar, a giant sandstone monolith, the names of these early explorers are scratched into the soft rock. Names like John Ross, the second explorer to cross the continent from south to north during the 1870 route-planning expedition for the Overland Telegraph Line, and W.M. Hayes and Mrs Hayes, who came this way in 1889.

The early explorers were followed by the miners who came north from South Australia in search of rare gemstones. The rubies they were looking for turned out to be garnets, but those who stayed began searching for gold. In 1887 they found alluvial deposits at Arltunga and, ten years later, reef gold was discovered in the nearby White Range. By the early 1900s, their dream – like the dreams of so many others in this strange land – disappeared, but today the old gold town at Arltunga, two hours drive from Alice Springs, has been restored and declared an historic reserve.

Alice Springs itself remains the heart of the Red Centre. Cradled at the foot of the MacDonnell Ranges, the town was founded by William Whitfield Mills in 1871 while he was surveying a route for the Overland Telegraph Line. He chose a dry river bed as the site for a telegraph repeater station and named it in honour of Sir Charles Todd, the South Australian Superintendent of Telegraphs. The nearby waterhole was named after his wife, Lady Alice.

Today's Alice might not be the New Yorkers' idea of sophistication, but in a land older than civilisation itself, the town is an oasis of comfort and charm and the unexpected. Just like the pioneers one hundred years ago, today's residents have learned to adapt to their environment. They even hold the Henley-on-Todd regatta here – in a dry river bed. The boats are bottomless and the crews stand inside. No one has to worry about wind shifts or sailpower as they scamper to the finishing line.

Here, perhaps more than anywhere else in Australia, the outback people have developed a grim humour and bold eccentricity for their situation. Their isolation is accepted and their fortitude has been passed down by the early explorers, many of whom now rest in the Old Pioneer Cemetery in George Crescent and the Alice Spring Cemetery in Memorial Drive. In the latter is the grave of Harold Lasseter, who died in the desert in 1931 while searching for 'Lasseter's Lost Reef' of gold.

Memories of those dramatic early pioneering days are recorded in Alice at places like the Old Timers' Museum on the Stuart Highway, the John Flynn Memorial Church and the Adelaide House and Radio Hut, where Australia's first Inland Mission Medical Centre opened in 1926. Here, too, is the home of the Royal Flying Doctor service, the brainchild of John Flynn, without which the people of the vast outback region of Australia would not be able to survive.

Yet for most visitors the biggest single attraction of the Centre remains the awesome sight of Ayers Rock, rising like a red shrine from the desert plain and mulga woodland of Uluru National Park. The Rock and the nearby Olgas are the peaks of otherwise buried rock masses which hold spiritual significance for the Aborigines of the Yankuntjatara and Pitjatjatjara tribes. Much of Central Australian Aboriginal mythology can be found in rock paintings and sacred sites which are now protected by the national park authorities. An Ayers Rock sunrise or sunset, when the colours of the sandstone change magically, is one of the greatest visual and spiritual experiences available to man.

Thirty kilometres away, the Olgas appear from the distance like giant marbles, arranged roughly in a circle rising up from the plain. This natural phenomenon – together with places like Standley Chasm, sheer cliff walls with an average width of fissure of around five metres – provide the traveller with breathtaking views.

Further north, in the Tablelands between the Centre and the Top End, past Barrow Creek (population eleven), is the gold-mining town of Tennant Creek, where in the 1920s men tried to hammer and chisel their fortunes out of granite outcrops. The Eldorado, largest of the early mines, closed down in 1958 after producing around 175,000 grams of gold.

At Kakadu National Park, 220km east of Darwin, there are some superb examples of Aboriginal art at Nourlangie Rock and Obiri Rock. The Jim Jim Falls (a 215-metre drop) and the Twin Falls are spectacular sights in an area of outstanding scenery.

Humid Darwin, bombed by Japanese planes in 1942 and devastated by the 250kph winds of Cyclone Tracey on Christmas Day, 1974, has shown its resilience by bouncing back as a bustling, cheerful tropical city. Darwin, one of the heaviest-drinking cities in the world, is the home of an annual boat race in which the craft are constructed entirely of beer cans. A condition of entry is that all the cans' contents must have been previously consumed by the crews.

Outback Australia is altogether a story about survival. The Aborigines who came and hunted for food, the explorers who came to unravel its secrets, and the stockmen, the drivers and the miners who followed the trail, have been united in their determination to accept the rigours and come back for more.

It is a bewitching wilderness. A land of the fearless and the foolhardy, the dreamer and the divine.

VICTORIA

Victoria ... the Garden State, but also, surely, the state of adventure, of fashion, good food and elegance.

Victoria's 277,620 square kilometres lie at the southeast corner of the Australian continent. It is the smallest of the mainland states, making up less than three per cent of Australia, but here, they will tell you with pride, it is quality and not quantity that counts. The climate may not be as good as it is on the west coast, but then a quarter of all people in Australia have decided that Victoria's forested mountains, wild coastline, rolling wheatlands and prosperous city living more than make up for the odd bout of inclement weather.

Victoria – and especially Melbourne, with its grand architecture – is outwardly more conservative than other Australian states, but don't be deceived, because under the cloak of formality is a vibrant, cosmopolitan world of high finance, fashion, carnival and good living. European in appearance, Melbourne – named after Queen Victoria's first prime minister – reflects the character and heritage of more than one hundred different cultures, brought here by people who have made their own special contributions to the style and pace of the city.

Gold first brought the migrants to Melbourne, and those who struck it rich in nearby fields began to build for themselves a city which would reflect their prosperity. In the 1880s, 'Marvellous Melbourne' was the place to be. The planners responded to the excitement of the era by designing on a lavish scale. Parks, gardens, wide boulevards and ornate architecture secured the city's future as the capital of stylish living.

It did not take long for the manufacturers, financiers and entrepreneurs to make their mark, and the foundations for long-term prosperity were laid. Today, Melbourne is the base for many of the nation's major financial institutions, which have seen no good reason to move away from a city which breathes good taste.

Yet buildings without people are bread without butter, and Melbourne's cosmopolitan mix has brought vitality, colour, excitement, new songs, dances, music and food to the city. More than 35 per cent of Melbourne's residents arrived as a result of post-Second World War migration, so don't be surprised if your vegetables are sold to you by a Greek, your meat by an Italian and your coffee by a Turk. These are just some of the people who have arrived from foreign lands to enrich this corner of Australia with their culture.

In its turn, the city has responded by providing its residents with a wonderful environment in which to live, particularly around the banks of the River Yarra, where walkers, cyclists, joggers and dreamers escape the city bustle. A fifth of the inner city area is given over to parkland and gardens, most of it within a short stroll of the commercial heart. The splendour of the Royal Botanic Gardens, 40 hectares of landscaped greenery, brings the gardens of the world to Melbourne's doorstep.

Despite the attractions of the city, few can resist the lure of the Dandenongs, 30 kilometres from Melbourne, where refuge is offered in picturesque little towns, country restaurants, picnic grounds and cosy tearooms serving Devonshire cream and scones. The Dandenongs is an endlessly fascinating region of giant trees, rhododendrons, tree ferns, leafy glades, lyre birds, parrots, the Puffing Billy narrow-gauge railway and historical buildings like the Edward Henty Cottage, home of the first permanent settler in Victoria, which today is furnished in the period of the 1850s, and classified by the National Trust. Here, too, is the William Ricketts Sanctuary, where dozens of hand-carved sculptures of Aboriginal faces peer out of the dense, green foliage. The Grampian Ranges, in the southwest of the state, provide a different panorama, with high plains giving way to the spectacular scenery of rugged peaks.

In Melbourne's bayside suburbs, the English influence is strong, and place names like Brighton, with its row of brightly-coloured, privately-owned bathing huts, Chelsea, Hampton and Sandringham – originally Gypsy Village but re-named in honour of the Royal Estate by the local landowner in 1888 – give clues to Victoria's historical links. Thomas Alexander Browne, author of 'Robbery Under Arms', and the poet Adam Lindsay Gordon are both buried in Brighton cemetery.

Further south, as Beach Road skirts Half Moon Bay, the scuttled *HMAS Cerberus*, ironclad flagship of the former Victorian Navy, now serves as a breakwater; and on the Mornington foreshore there is a cairn which marks the landing of Matthew Flinders, navigator and commander of *HMS Investigator*, on April 28, 1802. Mornington

Peninsula is Melbourne's holiday playground and it includes popular resorts like Rye and Rosebud, Dromana, Dorrento and Portsea. There is modern history here, too, for Australia's Prime Minister, Harold Holt, disappeared without trace while swimming at Cheviot Beach on December 17, 1967.

Across the entrance to Port Phillip Bay, the Bellarine Peninsula – and most especially Geelong, Victoria's second biggest city – was the favourite entry point for the prospectors who joined the gold rush to Ballarat in the 1850s. Now that turbulent era is immortalised in the reconstructed goldfield at Sovereign Hill. Geelong is an important city, recalling memories of the rich merchants' way of life in the 1850s at places like Barwon Grange, built for J.P. O'Brien, a merchant ship owner, and The Heights, a classic example of more than 100 buildings in Geelong and the surrounding area that have been classified by the National Trust. Industry dominates Geelong today, but for those who persevere there are still historical treasures to be found.

But there is more, much more, to Victoria. There is the magnificent Snowy River scenery which inspired the ballads of Banjo Patterson. There is the starkly-beautiful coastline and unique bushland of Wilson's Promontory. There is the rich grazing country of Gippsland and the expanse of the Gippsland Lakes, which form the largest inland waterways in Australia. There are wineries, historic towns, the winding Murray River with its paddle steamers and the majestic mountain resorts like Mt Hotham, Falls Creek, Mt Buffalo, Mt Buller and Mt Baw Baw. And, of course, there are the fairy penguins of Phillip Island, whose evening parade as they waddle out of the sea and across Summerland Beach is a magical sight.

But perhaps the trip around Victoria should finish back in Melbourne, at the Moomba – an Aboriginal word which, roughly translated, means 'let's get together and have fun.' Every March the festival attracts thousands of people from all over the state who want to do just that. The highlight, a three-hour street parade, is a Victorian celebration of their good fortune in being part of this glorious Garden City.

TASMANIA

Tasmania, a green speck slipping off a golden continent, is the other Australia. A land of strawberries and scallops, apples and alpine meadows, lavender and mountain lakes.

It is no bigger than England, a country with which, physically, it has so much in common. The hop fields, quaint fishing villages, leafy glades, tea shops, rhododendron gardens and old churches recall a more gracious age when people had time to enjoy the natural beauty around them.

In the dramatically beautiful southwest, the Last Wilderness has changed imperceptibly since the first Tasmanians sheltered in Kutikina and Deena Reena Caves on the Franklin River around 20,000 years ago. Forests occupy more that 40 per cent of Tasmania's land mass, and in the isolated southwest region man can but take tip-toe steps into the enchanting, hidden world of foaming rivers, rainforests, rapids and ravines, ancient Huon pine trees and alpine meadows flowing down from rugged, weather-beaten mountains.

The forests and rivers will share some of their secrets, but only with the most experienced bush-walkers or canoeists. No one can treat this area with anything other than total respect. The forests link this remote little island with the past, a time 37,000 years ago when marsupials, giant wombats and kangaroos roamed the swamps. Man followed some 17,000 years later at a time when the Bass Strait was exposed, allowing access from the mainland. Melting ice brought the floods which isolated Tasmania, allowing flora and fauna, extinct in other parts of the world, to flourish here. Huon and King Billy pines, blackwood, wattles and sassafras have given Tasmania its green-fringed canopy of splendour. The Tasmanian tiger, or thylacine, is thought to be extinct now, but the Tasmanian devil, an elusive, nocturnal animal, can still be sighted in the more remote bush areas.

More than anything else, the contrasts of Tasmania give it appeal and enchantment. The well-ordered, simple beauty of Hobart beneath the shadow of Mount Wellington; the shrouded stillness of the drowned Lake Pedder; the mosaic green and chocolate-brown countryside around Devonport; the fountains and Victorian bandstand of Launceston; the thermal pools and ferny glades of the Hartz Mountains; the English oaks and green lawns of Port Arthur ... these are some of the glories of Tasmania.

It was Abel Tasman who first discovered these riches in 1642 and claimed Van Diemen's Land – named in honour of the then governor of the Dutch East Indies – for Holland. Colonisation came later. The British, following a familiar pattern, moved in quickly when there were rumours about the French settling in southern Tasmania. An expedition under Lieutenant John Bowen set sail from Port Jackson, New South Wales, landing in Van Diemen's Land at Risdon, now a suburb of Hobart, on September 7th, 1803. His party of 49 included 24 convicts.

It was the beginning of a dark period of Tasmanian history. A penal settlement was established at Port Arthur, on the Tasman peninsula, in 1830, and 12,500 convicts endured an often brutal life here until they were transferred to Hobart in 1877. Connecting the peninsula to the mainland is a narrow strip of land, just 410 metres across, known as Eaglehawk Neck. Here the military rulers introduced a savage guard system, using dogs to prevent prisoners from escaping to the mainland.

The first railway in Australia ran from Taranna to Long Bay near Port Arthur, a distance of roughly 7km, and it was the convicts who were made to push the carriages along the line. Escape from the tyranny was near impossible – although Martin Cash and others managed it in 1843 – and many of the convicts and settlers who died were buried on the Isle of the Dead at the entrance to the bay at Port Arthur. The Isle of the Dead is the last resting place for more than 1,600 convicts and 200 free settlers and soldiers.

Today, peaceful Port Arthur and the beautiful areas of southeast Tasmania hold the memories of those harsh colonial days. Elegant Richmond, 26km from Hobart, contains Australia's oldest freestone road bridge, the Old Gaol and Court House, all built in the 1820s. At New Norfolk, founded by Norfolk Islanders in 1813, St Matthews Church is the oldest existing church building in Tasmania. The town is at the centre of an extensive rural area and anyone who has toured the hop fields of Kent, in England, will find a lot of similarities here.

Hobart, astride the lovely Derwent River, is Australia's second-oldest capital, and when the locals claim that it is one of the most beautiful harbour capitals in the world, there are few who would want to argue. The old colonial character of Hobart touches hands with modern-day Tasmania in streets like Salamanca Place, where old Georgian warehouses are now occupied by shops and restaurants, and Battery Point, the original seamen's quarters of the city.

Battery Point was named after a battery of guns placed on a promontory next to the present docks, to protect the settlement from the French. The guns were never used against invaders, but the powder magazine and signal station still exist. Many of the buildings from the original village are as they were in the 1830s and 1840s, along with some of the public houses which catered to the sea captains, merchants and fishermen who moved into the area in the middle of the last century. In Macquarie Street and Davey Street, too, the past is lovingly preserved, but amid all this colonial splendour Hobart has not stood still. The Wrest Point Casino in Sandy Bay, Australia's first casino, is proof that the city can look forward as well as back.

Beyond Hobart the rich seam of Tasmanian landscape spreads out around the Derwent as it flows through hop fields, ancient forests and green lawns. Mount Field National Park, 77km from Hobart, includes the famous 40-metre Russell Falls and, slightly further afield, the area around Lake Dobson provides a winter wonderland for skiers.

Inland from Hobart is little England, a land of apple and pear orchards, green pastures and vineyards. All this set against the snow-capped Hartz Mountains, where the national park was described by Sir Edmund Hilary as 'some of the wildest and most spectacular scenery I have ever seen.' Here your nostrils are filled with cool mountain air while your eyes feast on rainforests and alpine wildflowers. The blackjack tables and roulette wheels of Wrest Point seem a million miles away as nature spreads its own cards on the table.

The national parks are the emeralds in Tasmania's tiara. Ben Lomond, home of Tasmania's best skiing fields, Franklin and Lower Gordon, where the wild rivers run below the massive white quartzite peak of Frenchman's Cap; Cradle Mountain and Lake St Clair, Australia's deepest natural freshwater lake; Rocky Cape National Park, where the wildflowers, parrots and honeyeaters complete the kaleidoscope, and the South West National Park, largest in the state, where mountain peaks, glacial tarns, eucalypt forests and button grass plains lure the adventurer deeper into the wilderness.

History is everywhere in Tasmania. In the north, around the Tamar Valley, among the old homesteads and gold mining ruins; in Devonport at the Maritime Museum; in Launceston among the merchant warehouses, and along the unspoiled east coast beaches where the whalers once came.

Tasmania is a marvellous surprise wrapped up in a little package. It is Australia in a nutshell.

AUSTRALIAN CAPITAL TERRITORY
It might be easy to get sidetracked away from Canberra and the Australian Capital Territory by the sophistication of Sydney and the magic of Melbourne, but to ignore Australia's seat of government would be a mistake.

Of course, Canberra is neat and tidy. Of course, it is inland and has little colonial history to fall back on. Of course, it has no dusty nooks and crannies to add character, nor any ancient monuments to peer at. But every city needs time to find its place in the world, and Canberra has made massive strides since 1908 when it was selected as the site for the national capital. An American architect won the international competition to design the city, and in 1913 it was given its name after an Aboriginal word meaning 'meeting place.'

Parliament first met there in 1927, but the intervention of World War II slowed progress and it wasn't until well into the 1950s that the pace of Canberra really picked up. Latest figures show the population of the 2,366 square kilometres of Australian Capital Territory as 253,000, which is remarkable growth considering that, in 1960, the figure was around 55,000.

Canberra, today, is developing its own character, and there are fewer complaints these days of a city lacking soul – but not public servants! Twelve million trees and shrubs have provided colour; imposing embassy buildings have given it class. The artificial Lake Burley Griffin divides the city between the north, where residential areas proliferate, and the south, where the government buildings, including the National Gallery, the High Court and the National Library, are concentrated within the parliamentary triangle envisaged by its designer, Burley Griffin.

The apex of this triangle will be the new Parliament House. The 'temporary' old Parliament House will be retained and will no doubt become a tourist attraction to rank with the Australian War Memorial at the foot of Mount Ainslie. The museum has an enormous amount of war memorabilia – books, photographs, paintings, sketches and diaries – but perhaps its most impressive exhibit is one of the Japanese miniature submarines which slipped into Sydney Harbour during World War II. Canberra has tried both to collect history around it, particularly in the National Library, and to acknowledge it with the spectacular water memorial to Captain Cook.

The bonus for the people of Canberra is that they can have all this clean, uncluttered city living and still escape to the nearby Snowy Mountains when public service life gets too much for them. The National Library holds the Jindabyne Tapes, an oral history of the real men from Snowy River, immortalised in Banjo Patterson's famous ballad. Departing residents from the old town of Jindabyne, before it was submerged beneath Lake Jindabyne, were interviewed about the identity of the Man from Snowy River, and popular opinion held that Patterson had created his daring horseman from many of the real characters who galloped through the wild mountain ranges.

Today, though, Canberra is very much a living city, building its own history and its own legends.

NEW SOUTH WALES
Much has been written about the twin glories of Sydney – the stunning, sail-like concrete curves of the Opera House and the magnificent Harbour Bridge. And in all those words, no one has yet managed to overstate the stimulus it affords the senses. Those who have made comparisons between the compelling majesty of India's Taj Mahal and the awesome splendour of Joern Utzon's masterpiece on Bennelong Point are surely close to the mark when they claim that the Opera House, opened in 1973, 14 years after work began, is the eighth wonder of the world.

Sydney is a magical place, a sparkling, invigorating, string-of-pearls city. There is style and sophistication here. There is commercial vitality and cultural awareness. There is raffishness and there is ritz. There is history and there is hullabaloo. There is Bondi Beach and Harry's Cafe de Wheels in Woolloomooloo, Doyle's seafood restaurant at Watson's Bay, night-time Kings Cross, the famous Sydney cricket ground and the Victorian elegance of Paddington.

Australia's oldest, liveliest and most spectacular city has come a long way since Captain Cook passed by without stopping in 1770. Cook, poor fellow, anchored in Botany Bay, a few kilometres to the south, pausing briefly to name the vast expanse of Sydney Harbour in honour of George Jackson of the British Admiralty.

On Monday, January 26, 1788, Captain Arthur Phillip, commander of the first convict fleet, arrived in Botany Bay but moved on to Port Jackson because of its better anchorages and greater protection. The first settlers established themselves in Sydney Cove, where Circular Quay is today. The nearby Rocks area is an endlessly fascinating link with Australia's colonial past. The Rocks was the site of Australia's first prison, barracks and hospital and, although many of its buildings were pulled down during an outbreak of bubonic plague at the end of the last century, the area has been sympathetically restored.

The restored Cadman's Cottage, built in 1815, is Sydney's oldest existing building, and the Argyle Centre, convict-built in the 1820s, is now home to arts and crafts displays. If you need reminding of how tough life was for those early convicts, take a look at Argyle Cut and think what it must have been like, day after day for 16 years, as the prisoners gouged a passage out of the solid rock. The Rocks is where it all started, and today it is the best place to orientate yourself in this radiant city.

Spread out are the charms and surprises of a city which combines the best aspects – but few of the drawbacks (if you don't count the Harbour Bridge traffic jams) – of other great cities around the world. Sydney has a special atmosphere which can be sensed in a moment whilst sitting on a bench on the shores of Farm Cove reading a newspaper, listening to the Sunday afternoon speakers haranguing the crowds at the Domain, strolling through Kings Cross, taking a water taxi to Rose Bay, or listening to free entertainment in Martin Place.

Everybody is offered the opportunity of discovering what this city means to them. Whether it's the head-spinning panorama from the Manly ferry, the view over the entrance to Sydney Harbour from the top of the North Head, the lushness of the Botanical Gardens or the beautiful, bikini-clad girls on Bondi Beach, there is something here to suit every taste. From the plushness of Vaucluse, through the high style of Point Piper to the dazzling shopping delights of Double Bay, the cacophony of Kings Cross and the trendy charm of Paddington, this lucky city has come a long way in 200 years.

If, like me, you never tire of Sydney, you should remember that New South Wales has more to offer than a bridge and an opera house. There is the near-tropical north, the Snowy Mountains, 1,300 kilometres of outstanding coastline, and the marvellous Murray Riverina region, where inland Australia was pioneered by the settlers and then plundered by bushrangers like Ned Kelly, Mad Dan Morgan, Captain Moonlight and Frank Gardner.

The Murray Riverina includes the major cities of Albury and Wagga Wagga, the mighty waters of the 2,600-kilometre Murray and the 1,700-kilometre Murrumbidgee (an Aboriginal word meaning 'big water'), the little townships of Corowa and Mulwala and Wentworth, the latter situated near the junction of the Murray and the Darling, Australia's second largest and second most important river.

This is the old bandit country where, in 1879, Ned Kelly held up the local police station and robbed the bank at Jerilderie, and where the notorious Captain Moonlight was tried in Gundagai's 1859 court house. Gundagai's other famous monument is a sculpture of the celebrated dog who, in the bush ballad 'sat on the tuckerbox, five miles from Gundagai.' There's Hay, where Cobb and Co. built their coaches, and Hell, where you find the One Tree Pub, and there's the Merriwagga Black Stump bar, tallest in the land, where thirsty horsemen could take a beer without leaving the saddle.

The Riverina is an outstanding area, both for its historical associations, its legends, its superb river playgrounds and for the Murrumbidgee Irrigation System which has transformed the area west of the Snowy Mountains into a flourishing land of vineyards, cotton fields, orchards and rolling green pastures. Henry Lawson, asked by the government to write about the virtues of the new irrigation scheme, penned a letter to a friend in 1916 in which he told of 'a spread of green, all chequered off, with little homes and trees and clear, green-fringed canals and channels, just like English brooks, set in a midst of a bare-scorching dusty red and parched yellow Dead Land that's a lot older than Egypt.'

The Murray was discovered by the explorers Hume and Hovell during an ambitious overland trip from Sydney to Melbourne in 1824. Six years later, Captain Charles Sturt 'rediscovered' it and changed its name from the Hume to the Murray after a British Colonial Secretary. Hume had to be content with his name on the highway linking Australia's two largest cities. The Murray region is irrigated by the waters of the Snowy Mountains, the roof of Australia, where Mt Kosciusko towers majestically to 2,238 metres.

James Spencer lived here in the rugged mountain country in the 1840s, and his exploits as a daring horseman, stockman and pioneer are believed to have been the inspiration for Banjo Paterson's famous ballad, 'The Man from Snowy River'. Paterson listened to the campfire tales of the old stockmen of the Snowy and wove the characters of their stories into his own ballads. The high passes and treeless valleys no longer echo to the hoofbeats of the flying horses. Today, up among the snowdrifts, it is the swish of skis that ruffles the brilliant white blanket of the Snowys.

Away from Sydney, the Murray Riverina and the Snowy Mountains, New South Wales has still more to offer. The magnificent wines of the Hunter Valley, Australia's largest iron and steel works at Newcastle, the 'Silver City' of Broken Hill, the high plateau of the New England region, the sweeping beaches of the north coast towards Queensland and the secret bays and inlets of the south.

Simply, it's a great state to get into.

QUEENSLAND

Queensland – the Sunshine State – lays claim to being Australia's premier holiday destination. It is big, boisterous and brash. Yet, at times, it can be quirkily conservative in a way which can put it out of step with the rest of the country. This is not to say that Queenslanders are any less friendly or less hospitable than their fellow Australians. You will be welcomed just as warmly in your travels around this state of surprise.

Within its 1.7 million square kilometres, Queensland is a land of striking contrasts: of outback desert and tropical rainforest, of rugged mountains and endless flat plains, of surfing beaches and baked salt pans, of historic towns and modern high-rise resorts, of kangaroos and crocodiles. But, for the majority of Australians, and for that matter many overseas visitors, Queensland is the Gold Coast and the Great Barrier Reef.

The Gold Coast – a 50-kilometre strip tucked into the southeast corner of Queensland – is a high-rise holiday playground based around sand, sun and surf. It is a heady mix – the English seaside resort of Brighton, Spain's Costa del Sol and California's Disneyland all rolled into one. It is blousy and brazen, gaudy and glamorous, a lucky dip of candyfloss fun and caviar good living. The Gold Coast is a mecca for the beautiful people who have turned it into Australia's holiday capital. And, if the Gold Coast is not to everyone's taste, it makes no apologies. Tourism is the reason the Gold Coast was created, and the city fathers will tell you they are simply providing what the visitors want. The endorsement of this policy lies in the three million plus tourists who annually visit the coastal strip. And the thousands of 'southerners' who each year migrate north to spend their retirement years enjoying life in this balmy, sub-tropical paradise.

Further up the coast is the jewel in Queensland's tourism crown, the marine wonderland of the Great Barrier Reef. The reef, stretching for more than 2,000 kilometres along the eastern coastline of Queensland, is formed by more than 350 varieties of exotically-coloured live coral. Surely no other place in the world can offer snorkellers and scuba divers such a fantastic underwater experience. Fish of every size and hue dart among the fascinating coral formations.

But you don't have to don a wet suit to enjoy this technicolour extravaganza. Queensland's tourism operators have developed craft which allow you to explore the reef without getting your toes wet. Townsville entrepreneur Doug Tarca was the first to introduce a semi-submersible craft to the reef. This innovative Queenslander developed the boat because he wanted everyone – young, old, fit and disabled – to share in the magic of the reef. His yellow submarine, called the *Manta*, is moored to a pontoon on the John Brewer Reef some 72 kilometres from Townsville. You get there from the mainland on a giant 250-seat catamaran, a high speed journey which includes a succulent seafood and salad buffet lunch. Once at the reef, you board the *Manta* (it takes up to 50 passengers) for a fascinating encounter with the myriad forms of marine life and the colourful coral.

If the Great Barrier Reef is the state's crown, then the many islands dotted along the coast are her jewels. These are the idyllic islands of which dreams are made – swaying palms, brilliant white sandy beaches, secluded coves, sleepy reef-protected bays, lush vegetation, exotic fruits and equally exotic birds and flowers.

There are few places on earth to match the Whitsunday Islands for enchanting beauty. They lie between the rainforested hills of the Whitsunday coast and the coral ribbon of the Great Barrier Reef. You can cruise through the Whitsunday Passage, anchoring by an uninhabited island to go scuba diving and snorkelling in the turquoise waters. You can charter cruisers, sail on crewed yachts, sign on for island-hopping camping cruises or join a sophisticated cruise boat.

If you're a confirmed landlubber, then there is a choice of island resorts where you can enjoy a pampered, carefree existence. Try Hamilton Island, where an international standard resort has been created to cater for the pleasure seekers who want five-star facilities on their island retreat. Or Daydream Island. Or Hayman Island. Or Lindeman Island. Or Brampton Island. Or one of the numerous other resort islands strung along the coast, each enticing you with their special charms.

Queensland's picturesque coastal towns and inland centres can be full of surprises, too. Places like Bundaberg, a major sugar-producing centre and home of the famous local rum of the same name. The town also has a niche in history as the home of the pioneer aviator Bert Hinkler, who made the first epic solo flight between England and Australia in 1928.

Places like Mon Repos Beach, where three kinds of turtle come ashore each year to lay their eggs. Places like historic Gayndah, inland from Bundaberg and one of the oldest towns in the state, or Kilkivan, where you can fossick for gemstones, and the volcanic crater lakes in the Coulston Lakes National Park. Places like Winton, a town of 1,300 people on the Rockhampton to Mt Isa road. It was on a station near Winton that Australia's celebrated poet-songwriter Banjo Patterson wrote his now famous ditty, Waltzing Matilda. And it was here, too, that Australia's international airline, Qantas, had its humble beginnings.

Places like Townsville, the third largest city in Queensland, with a population of 80,000. This port city serves the vast mineral- and agriculturally-rich hinterland of northern Queensland. From the dominating landmarks of Castle Hill you get splendid panoramic views of the city and across to Magnetic Island. Townsville has many charming old buildings and an excellent mall full of interesting shops where you can browse and, if the fancy takes you, buy. Or you can simply sit back and watch the others having a good time. Places like Nerada, where you can visit Australia's only tea plantation and climb Mt Bartle Frere, Queensland's highest mountain.

And Cairns, the major centre in Queensland's tropical far north. A relaxed, friendly city which marks the end of the Bruce Highway and the railway line from Brisbane. From here you can visit Green Island, a delightful coral cay resort, venture north into the wilderness area of the Cape York Peninsula, or explore the magnificent rainforest areas of the Atherton Tableland. Highly recommended is the scenic train ride from Cairns through breathtaking Barron Gorge up into the mountains to Kuranda, a journey of 35 kilometres. Kuranda itself is a cool, green, tropical delight of native shrubs, ferns and flowers.

Port Douglas, north of Cairns, is also well worth visiting. It is a picture postcard town with many fine old buildings, interesting little shops and restaurants and a truly superb beach. This once quiet fishing hamlet has been discovered by the wider world and is now a thriving tourist destination.

There are many tough mining towns and remote communities in the interior. Probably, the most famous of these is Birdsville, the end of civilisation before you head off along the Birdsville track across the forbidding Simpson Desert into South Australia. For fairly obvious reasons, it's the Birdsville Pub which has given this tiny settlement of 200 hardy inhabitants a special place in Australian folklore. Here you buy your last draught beer for hundreds of kilometres or, alternatively, slake your thirst if you've come the other way.

The capital of this state of contrasts and colour is Brisbane, Australia's third largest city, with a population of 1.25 million. Situated in the southeast corner of the state, close to the New South Wales border, Brisbane has a distinct tropical feel about it, particularly on balmy summer nights when the warm, moist air gently hugs you.

To many overseas visitors Brisbane, probably more than any other capital, is likely to fit their image of an Australian city. The city skyline, unlike Sydney and to a lesser extent Melbourne, is not dominated by rows of office towers, and it still retains the atmosphere, if not quite the appearance, of a big country town. There is a strong Australian influence in much of its architecture, particularly in the suburbs. It is not uncommon to see houses with wide verandahs under corrugated iron roofs, and weatherboard houses perched on stilts to let the air circulate underneath and provide some respite from the intense summer heat.

Brisbane is a charming, gentle city with a friendly, warm smile; a city where you feel welcome and comfortable rather than lonely and intimidated.

This, then, completes our brief tour of a continent of, above all, contrasts – at once awe-inspiring and welcoming, forbidding and friendly. A land that, whilst reflecting the origins of its inhabitants, still retains the unique qualities that the very name – Australia – evokes.

Darwin Above: Diamond Beach Hotel Casino.   Below: Vestys Beach.

Above: Smith Street.   Below: Government House.

15

Darwin Above: lush vegetation near Darwin.   Below: the Reserve Bank of Australia.

Below: the law courts.

Below: Diamond Beach Hotel Casino.

Below: Joss House at the Chinese Temple

Above: antennae outside the A.B.C. studios in Cavenagh Street.

Above: sulphur being unloaded at Stokes Hill Wharf.　　Right: the grounds of the Reserve Bank of Australia.

Below: a ship docked at Fort Hill Wharf.

Below: Christchurch Anglican Cathedral.

Below: Joss House at the Chinese Temple.

Above: Fogg Dam marshlands, near Darwin.

Below: a saltwater crocodile.

Above and below: the Fogg Dam bird observatory near Darwin.

19

Above: a route across the outback.

Above: Fogg Dam marshland.

Below: a water buffalo.

Above: an esturine crocodile in Kakadu National Park.   Below: Katherine Gorge.

Below: Berry Springs, Darwin.

Above: the Adelaide River.

Above: Ormiston Gorge and Pound National Park in the Red Centre.

Below: a bush fire.

Above: road train at the Shell Roadhouse, Dunmarra.

Below: Tennant Creek.

Below: kangaroos in the animal compound of the Old Telegraph Station.

Below: a barbecue on Hamilton Downs near Alice Springs.

Below and right: the gymkhana barbecue on Hamilton Downs.

Above: Mataranka Pool Reserve.

Above: road train at the Shell Roadhouse, Dunmarra.

Above: Civic Centre in Tennant Creek.   Below: gymkhana on Hamilton Downs.

Above: a comprehensive signpost at Tennant Creek (below).

Alice Springs Above: the Church of the Lady of the Sacred Heart.

Above: Todd Street.

Above: the Old Telegraph Station.

Left: the Anzac Hill War Memorial.

Above and below: the Old Telegraph Station.

Below: the Old Telegraph Station.

Below: the Control Station of the Royal Flying Doctor Service.

Above: Aboriginal woman making fire. Below: Emily Gap, east of Alice Springs.

Above: Palm Valley Reserve. Below: Aboriginal boy.

Below: Palm Valley Reserve.

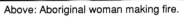

Below: a tour bus in the Palm Valley Reserve.

Above: Aboriginal woman looking for witchetty grubs. Below pictures: scenes from Aboriginal life near Alice Springs.

Below: clay sculptures by William Ricketts on the Pitchi-Richi Sanctuary.

Above: Ellery Creek.

Above: Ormiston National Park.

Above: Standley Chasm, West Macdonnell Ranges.

Above, below and left: Ayers Rock, Uluru National Park.

Above: Ormiston National Park.

Below: Standley Chasm, West Macdonnell Ranges.

Below: the Olgas, or 'Katatjuta', in Uluru National Park.

29

Above: Ayers Rock in Uluru National Park.

Below: the Olgas.

Below: the Olgas, or 'Katatjuta', in Uluru National Park.

33

Above: the Stock Exchange Arcade in Charters Towers.

Above: the Imperial Hotel, Ravenswood.

Above: fossicking for gemstones in the Rubyvale area.

Below: the Railway Hotel, Ravenswood.

Above: Ravenswood. Below: gem sifting near Rubyvale.

Below: the Australian Bank of Commerce, Charters Towers.

Below: Stock Exchange Arcade.

Below: Gill Street in Charters Towers.

Above: stock at Springsure.

Above: cotton plants and ginnery at Emerald.

Above: Blair Athol's open-cast coal pit at Clermont.

Above, below and left: fossicking for gems at Rubyvale.

Below: a 'road train' cattle transporter at Springsure.

33

Above: counting sheep, Silver Hills Inland Resort.   Below: the shearing shed at Silver Hills Inland Resort.

Above, below and right: Silver Hills Inland Resort.

Below: brewing a billy.

Below: Mount Isa Rodeo.

Above: cattle awaiting shipment in stockyards at Springsure.

Below: Mount Isa Rodeo.

Below: Fairbairn Reservoir at sunset.

Above: Mount Isa Rodeo.

Above and below: Mount Isa Rodeo, held every August.

Below: Mount Isa Rodeo.

Below: Mount Isa Rodeo. Below: cotton plants at Emerald, Central Queensland Highlands.

Above: Cairns.

Above: a harbour, Cairns.

Above: tea at the Narinda Plantation, near Cairns.

Below: a beach in the Cairns area.

Above: a banana plantation outside Cairns.

Below: the marina, Cairns.

Below: a banana crop outside Cairns.   Below: a harbour in Cairns.

Above: the marina at Cairns.

Great Barrier Reef Above: coral.

Above: a cleaner wrasse removing parasites.　　　　Below: coral.

Above: divers preparing to explore the Reef underwater.　　　　Below: a coral cay.

Below: a sea urchin crab.

Below: a beaked coralfish.

Below: coral.

Below: a reef crab feeding on algae.

Great Barrier Reef Above: a sea urchin (*Echinoidea*).   Below: a mauve ascidian.

Below: a sea star.

Above: a many-lined sweetlips.

Below: a crown-of-thorns sea star.   Above: Heron Island.

Above: a giant trumpet shell (*Claronia tritonis*).

Above: an orange band coral fish.

Above: a purple queen fish.

Below: a flatworm.

Above: a ragged-finned turkey fish.

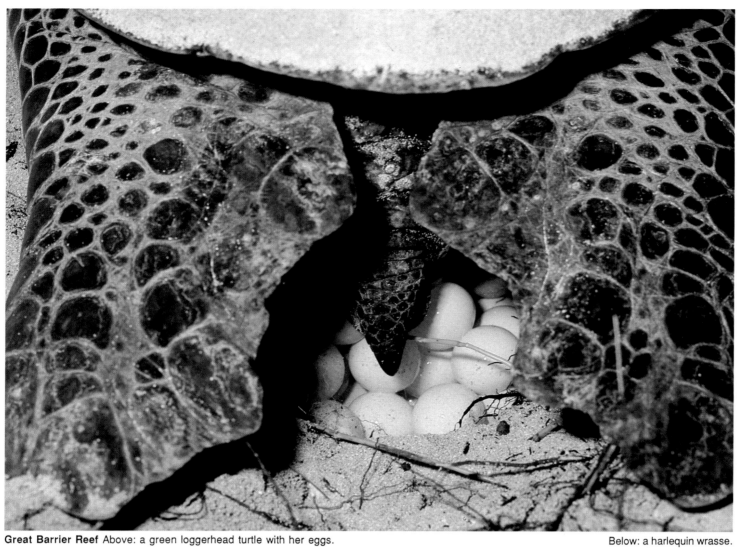

Great Barrier Reef Above: a green loggerhead turtle with her eggs.

Below: a harlequin wrasse.

Below: a coral cod.

Right: a sea urchin crab.

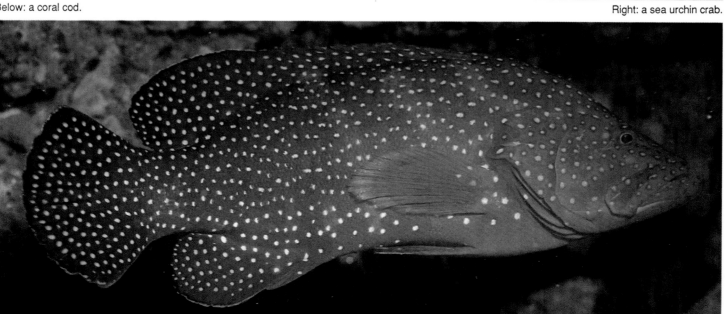

Above: bottlenosed dolphins.

Above: a hawksbill turtle.

Below: a sea star (*Asteroidea*).

Above: a white tip reef shark.

Above: a volute (*Amoria maculata*).

Above: a feather star.

Below: a rainbow runner.

45

Above: the Grand Hotel, Wooroolin.

Above: Rosslyn Harbour, near Yeppoon.   Below: Great Keppel Island.

Above: the Ballanjui Falls.

Above: the Queensland National Hotel in Mount Morgan.

Below left: Malanda Falls.   Below: Millaa Millaa Falls in the Atherton Tableland.

Above: boom netting off Great Keppel Island.　　Above right: Sunshine Pineapple Plantation.

Below: the 'Singing Ship' memorial to Captain Cook, near Yeppoon.

Above: Sugar Cane Train on the Sunshine Pineapple Plantation.　　Below: Heritage Tavern, Rockhampton.

Below: Kuranda Railway Viaduct, north of Cairns.

47

Brisbane Above: Anzac Square.

Below: Story Bridge.

Above: the city skyline across the Brisbane River.

Below: King George Square.

Brisbane Above: the Tropical Display Dome at the Botanic Gardens.

Below: Captain Cook Bridge.

Above: the Empire Hotel.

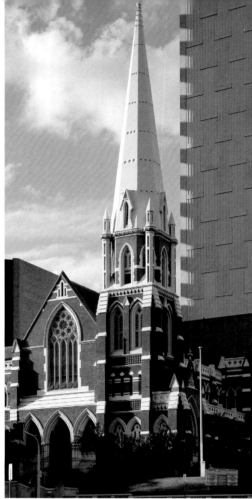

Above: Albert Street Methodist Church.

Below: Brisbane seen from Story Bridge at Petrie Bight.

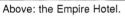

Below: Queen Street Mall.

Below: the Botanic Gardens, overlooked by Parliament House.

The Gold Coast

The Gold Coast

Above and below: Sea World, Southport.

Below: Sea World, Southport.

Above: giant chess at Surfers Paradise.

Below: Surfers Paradise shopping centre.

Above: a beach near Coffs Harbour.   Below: Tacking Point Lighthouse.

Above: banana plantation, Coffs Harbour.

Below: Trail Bay Gaol, Port Macquarie.

Below: banana plantation, Coffs Harbour.

Above: banana plantation, Coffs Harbour.   Below: Clarence Street, Port Macquarie.

Above: Korora Beach.

Below: Coffs Harbour.

Above: Ellenborough Falls, Bulea Plateau.

Below: Newcastle.

Below: Shelley Beach, near Fort Ma

Below pictures: Timbertown, near Wauchope.

Above: steam train at Timbertown, near Wauchope.

Above: The Entrance, north of Sydney.

Above: horses near Port Macquarie.   Below: Timbertown.

Below: fishing boat, Nelson Bay.

rie.   Below: Narrabeen, north of Sydney.

Above and below: Sydney Opera House.

Sydney Above: Manly Beach.   Below: Sydney skyline.

Below: Tamarama Beach.

Below: Sydney Opera House and Sydney Harbour Bridge.

60

Above: sightseeing, Sydney Harbour.

Above: Sydney Opera House.   Below: Pier 1.

Below: Sydney Opera House.

Above: the Royal Viking Star at Sydney Cove Terminal, Circular Key West.

Above: Sydney Opera House and Sydney Harbour Bridge.

Sydney Above: Centrepoint Tower.   Below: Sydney Opera House.

Above: Sydney Harbour Bridge and ferry.

Below: Bronte Beach.　　Below: harbourside apartments.

Sydney Above: the Rocks and central Sydney.   Below: buildings on Pitt Street.   Below: the Phillip Fountain.

Below: the Conservatorium of Music.

64

Above: Sydney Opera House.

Below: Harbord.

Sydney Above: Macquarie Street.

Below: Sydney Harbour.

Below: swimming pools.

Above: Pier 1.

Below: the El Alamein Fountain in Kings Cross.

Above: Sydney Harbour Bridge.

Sydney Above: Centrepoint Tower.

Below: a view towards Long Point.

Above: a brown bear, Taronga Park Zoo, Sydney.

Above: a dingo, Taronga Park Zoo.

Above: a koala.

Above: a kangaroo

Above: an echidna.   Below: a Tasmanian Devil, Taronga Park Zoo.

Above: a cassowary, Taronga Park Zoo.   Below: a peacock.

Above: Wentworth Falls, Blue Mountains.

Below: Weeping Rock.

Above: the Three Sisters, seen from Echo Point.

Below: Grand Arch.

Below: Scenic Skyway in the Blue Mountains.

Above: the Courthouse, Bathurst.

Above: George Street, Bathurst.   Below: Mount Panorama Motor Racing Circuit, Bathurst.

Above: St Stanislaus' College, Bathurst.

THE AUSTRALIAN POET
ANDREW BARTON PATERSON
(BANJO)
WAS BORN 17TH FEB'Y. 1864 AT THE
NARRAMBLA HOMESTEAD WHICH
STOOD 8 CHAINS NORTH-EAST OF
THIS MEMORIAL.
ERECTED 1947
"AND HE SEES THE VISION SPLENDID
OF THE SUNLIT PLAINS EXTENDED,
AND AT NIGHT THE WONDROUS GLORY
OF THE EVERLASTING STARS"
(CLANCY OF THE OVERFLOW)

Above: a memorial in Orange.

Below: Duntryleague Country Club near Bathurst.

Above: Carcoar.   Below: George Street, Bathurst.

Above: the Civic Centre, Bathurst.

Above: Main Street, Orange.

Below: Machattie Park, Bathurst.

Dubbo Above: the War Memorial.

Above: Macquarie Street

Above: an elephant and (below) camels, Western Plains Zoo.

Above: a koala, Western Plains Zoo.

Left, above and below: Old Dubbo Gaol.

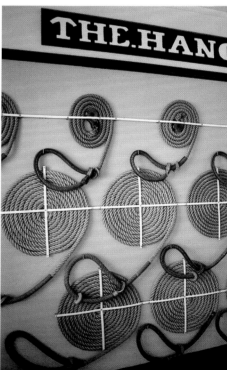

Above: Macquarie Street.

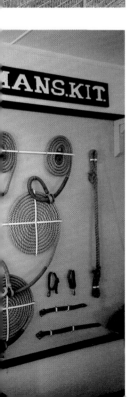

Above: a tiger and (below) chital deer, Western Plains Zoo.

Below: North American bison, Western Plains Zoo.

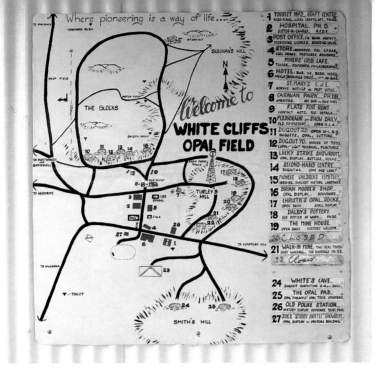

Above: copper mining, Cobar.

Above: opal mining, White Cliffs.

Above: Post Office, Broken Hill.

Above: Sulphide Street Railway Station, Broken Hill.

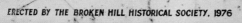

WHITE ROCKS - THE TURKS LAST STAND

ON JANUARY 1ST 1915 A PICNIC TRAIN TRANSPORTING 1200 PASSENGERS TO SILVERTON WAS FIRED UPON BY TWO TURKS AS IT REACHED THE OUTSKIRTS OF BROKEN HILL. THE TURKS THEN RAN TOWARDS THE OUTCROP KNOWN AS WHITE ROCKS WHERE, AGAINST AN ARMED FORCE OF MILITIA, POLICE & CIVILIANS, THEY MADE A LAST STAND. FOUR PEOPLE WERE KILLED & SEVEN WOUNDED BY THE TURKS, WHO FINALLY MET THEIR DEATH IN THIS AREA. TURKEY WAS AN ALLY OF GERMANY IN WORLD WAR I, & THIS INCIDENT MARKED THE ONLY ENEMY ATTACK ON AUSTRALIAN SOIL DURING THE FIRST WORLD WAR.

ERECTED BY THE BROKEN HILL HISTORICAL SOCIETY, 1976

Above: landscape near Broken Hill.

Below: Broken Hill.

Below: Council Administrative Centre, Broken Hill.

Below: Barrier Highway.

Above and below: landscape near White Cliffs.

Above and below: Silverton gaol.

Above and below: Silverton.

Below: Silverton.

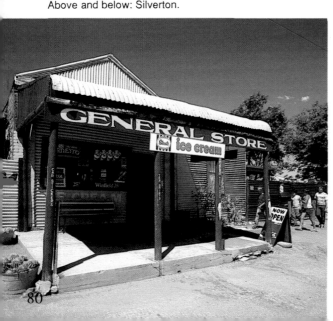

Below: control centre for NSW Flying Doctor Service.

Below: plane of the NSW Flying Doctor Service.

Above: confluence of the Murray and Darling rivers, near Wentworth.

Above, below and right: grape cultivation, Murrumbidgee Irrigation Area.

Below: grape drying in the Wentworth area.

Below: vineyard, Murrumbidgee Irrigation Area, near Griffith.

Above and right: outback horses northwest of Darling.

Above, below, above right and right: grape cultivation in the Murrumbidgee Irrigation Area, near Griffith.

Below: houseboat near Wentworth.

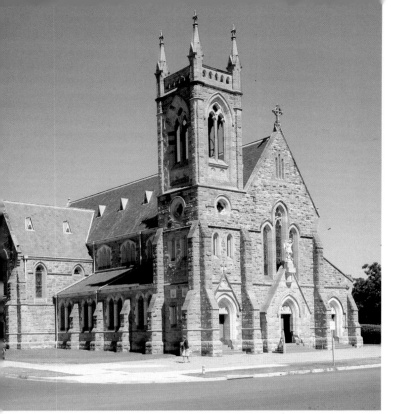

Above: St Michael's Catholic Cathedral, Wagga Wagga.

Above and below: Murrumbidgee Irrigation Area.

Above: Civic Theatre, Wagga Wagga.

Above: Banner Avenue and (below) Memorial Gardens, Griffith.

Below: Wagga Wagga.

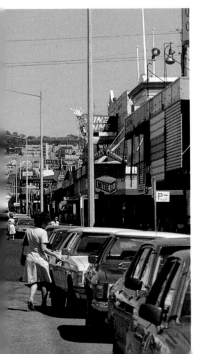

Above and below: Riverina area, near Narrandera.

Below: a bank in Narrandera.

Above: Parliament House.

Canberra Above: the Australian War Memorial.

Above and below: Australian National Gallery and Sculpture Garden.

Above: the Sculpture Garden.

Below: National Library.

Below: Parliament House.

Below: Parliament House.

Canberra Above: National Sports Centre.　　　Below: National Indoor Sports Centre.

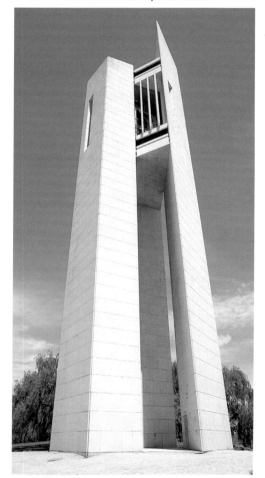

Above: the Canberra Carillon.　　　Below: Lake Burley Griffin.　　　Below: Australian War Memorial.

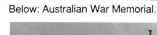

Above: All Saints Church, Ainslie.

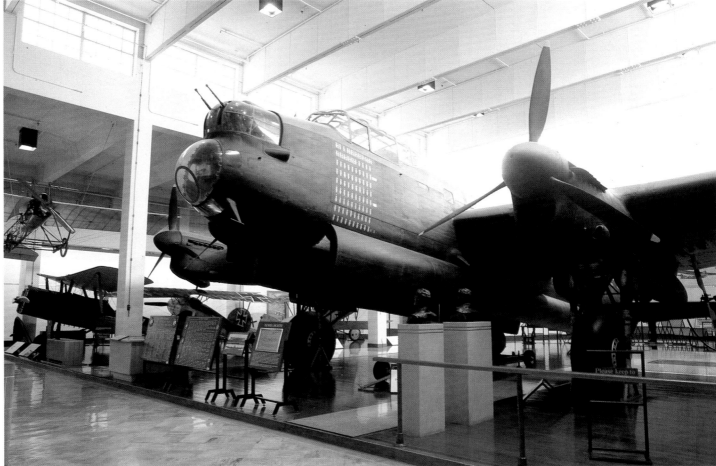

Above: Australian War Memorial exhibit.

Below: National Indoor Sports Centre.

Canberra Above: Blundell's Farmhouse. Below: Captain Cook Memorial, Lake Burley Griffin.

Above: Sculpture Garden.

Below: Lanyon.

Above: the Swimming Centre.

Below: telecommunications tower on Black Mountain.

Above: Canberra Deep Space Communication Complex, Tidbinbilla.

Below: Mount Stromlo Observatory.

Above and below: Perisher Valley in the Snowy Mountains.

Above: the Man from Snowy River, Cooma.

Above: the Thredbo Hotel, Snowy Mountains.

FIRE DANGER TODAY

LOW MODERATE HIGH VERY HIGH EXTREME

NO FIRES WITHOUT A PERMIT

SNOWY-TUMUT DEVELOPMENT

SNOWY-MURRAY DEVELOPMENT

Below: trout sculpture at Adaminaby.

Above: Batemans Bay.

Below: McKenzies Beach.

Below: coal at Wollongong Docks.

Below: Wollongong Marina.

Above: Stanwell Park, north of Wollongong.   Below: Clyde River Bridge.

Above: Bellerive, a suburb of Hobart.

Hobart Above: Wrest Point Marina and Casino.

Below: Hobart seen from the slopes of Mount Nelson.

Below: Tasman Bridge.

Hobart Below: Tasman Bridge and Mount Wellington.

Below: Hobart Botanical Gardens.

Below: Elizabeth Street Mall.

Below: Victoria Dock and the Customs House.

Above: the fishing port of Dover.

Above: landscape of western Tasmania.

Below: Queenstown.

Below: Russell Falls, Mount Field National Park.

Above: Lake Gordon and the Gordon Dam. Below: Strahan in Macquarie Harbour.

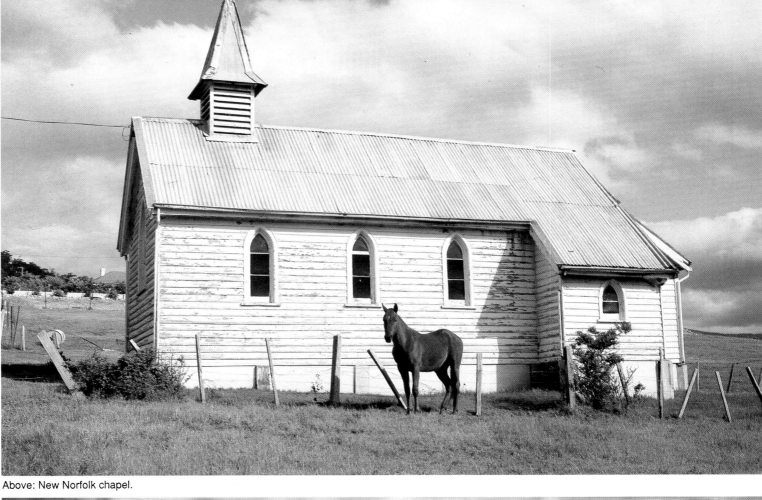

Above: New Norfolk chapel.

Above: a Tasmanian devil.

Below: Dover Harbour.

Above: Penguin.

Above: John Hart Conservatory.

Below: Gunpowder Mill, Penny Royal Complex.

Below: Launceston.

Above: farmland at Burnie.

Above: boats on the Tamar River.

Above: Devonport Lighthouse.

Above: Cataract Gorge.   Below: Launceston.

Above: Richmond Jail.

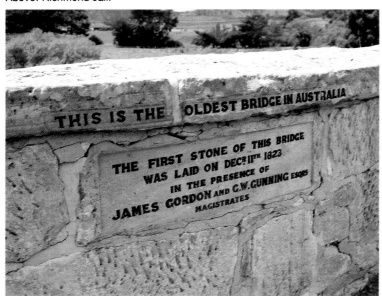

Below: Scamander.

Below: countryside near Springfield.

Left and above: Richmond Bridge.

Above: coastline near Mayfield.

Above: Port Arthur Asylum.

Above: Port Arthur Penitentiary.

Above: church and (below) fishing boats, Port Arthur.

Below: Branxholm.

Above: Island Archway, Port Campbell National Park.

Below: Razorback Rock, Port Campbell National Park.

Left: Split Point Lighthouse.   Below: Broken Head, Port Campbell National Park.

106

Above: lighthouse at Point Lonsdale.

Above: the post office at Geelong.

Below: the Arch, Port Campbell National Park.

Below: Bridgewater Bay.

Above: Mildura Workingman's Club.

Above: Liebig Str

Above: Deakin Avenue, Mildura.

Below: riverboat

Below: Flagstaff Hill, near Warrnambool.

arrnambool.

Above: Flagstaff Hill, near Warrnambool.

Murray River.

Above: Portland.

Below: Hamilton.

111

Above: the Mall, Bendigo.

Below: Joss House, Bendigo.

Above and below: Echuca.

Below: a winery near Red Cliffs.

Above: Swan Hill Pioneer Settlement.

Above: Echuca.

Above: the Shamrock Hotel, Bendigo.   Below: Bendigo.

Above: Puffing Billy in the Dandenongs.

Remaining pictures: Sovereign Hill, Ballara

Melbourne Zoo Above: a kookaburra.

Above: a heron.   Below: a gorilla.

Above: gorillas.

Above: pelicans.

Below: a masked plover.

Below: a heron.

Above: a banded land-rail.   Below: a kangaroo.

114

Above: meerkats.

Below: tree kangaroos.

Above: wallabies.

Below: an orang utan.

Above: a parrot.

Below: gibbons.

Below: a kangaroo with joey.

Below: macaws.

Melbourne Below: a Melbourne tram.

Below: Princes Bridge.

Below: Saint Patrick's Cathedral.

Above: Melbourne trams.

Below: Flinders Street Station.

Above: rowing on the River Yarra.

Below: a Melbourne tram.

Above: Exhibition Building.

Melbourne Below: Little Bourke Street.   Above: City Square.   Below: Brighton Beach.

Above: Saint Paul's Cathedral.

Below: Victorian Arts Centre.

Above: Flinders Street Station.

Below: James Cook's cottage.

Below: Brighton Beach.

Below: Parliament of Victoria building.

119

Melbourne Above: Wellington Parade.

Below: Bourke Street Mall.

Above: the Yarra River, near Princes Street Bridge.

Above: a Melbourne beach.

Below: the Australian Open.

Melbourne Cup Day.

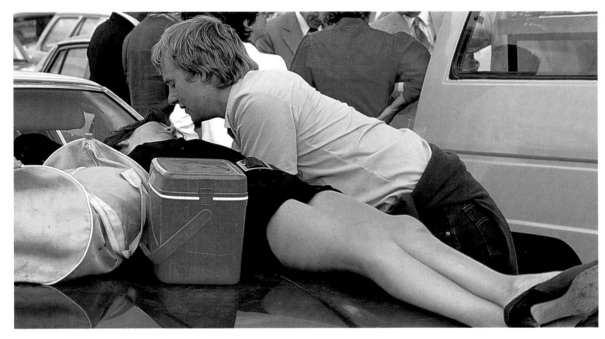

Above: Mount Buffalo National Park.

Below: Bulga National Park.

Above: Tanswell's Hotel, Beechworth.

Below: Pyramid Rock, Phillip Island.

Above: Wangaratta.   Below: Ned Kelly's home, Glenrowan.

Below: Squeaky Beach, Wilsons Promontory National Park.

Below: Myrtleford Bowls Club.

Below: reconstruction of Ned Kelly's childhood home at Glenrowan.

Below: a fairy penguin.

Adelaide Above: the Oval cricket ground.

Below: the Governor's Residence.

Below: sunset at Glenelg beach.

Above: Rundle Shopping Mall.

Adelaide Above, below and right: the Torrens River.

Below: the Botanic Hotel.

Above and below: the Festival Centre.

Below: Hindmarsh Square.

Above: Elder Park's bandstand.

Below: the Festival Centre.

Above: Barossa Valley.   Below: Moonta.

Below: Wallaroo.

Below: the Kaiser Stuhl cellars in Nuriootpa, Barossa Valley.

Above and below: locally-produced fruit near Berri, Barossa Valley.

Below: Tanunda.

Below: Chateau Yaldara.

Above: chateau in the Barossa Valley.

Above: pruning vines near Barmera. Below: church in the Barossa Valley.

Below: Barossa Valley agricultural land.

Below: Morphett Vale, near Adelaide.

Below: wine cellars in the Barossa Valley district.

Above: Coober Pedy.

Above: underground church, Coober Pedy.   Below: Port Augusta.

Below: Ceduna.

Below: truck at Kiruba.

Below: camels near Port Augusta.

Below: Coober Pedy.

Above: road near Whyalla.

Above and below: Port Augusta.

Above and below: Port Augusta.

Below: overseas telecommunications at Ceduna station.

Below: gypsum for export from Ceduna.

133

Above: the Pinnacles.

Above: Cape Naturaliste.

Below: War Memorial, King's Park, Perth.

Below: Wave Rock, near Hyden.

Below: Kalbarri National Park.

Above: land between Wittenoom and Hamersley Gorge.

Below: the bush north of Perth.

Perth Above: the Swan River.

Above: central Perth.

Below: Hay Street Mall.

Perth Above: central Perth beyond King's Park.

Below: Malcolm Street.

Above: St. Mary's Roman Catholic Cathedral, Victoria Square.

Below: Hay Street M

Above: Bayley Street, Coolgardie.

Above and below: Kalgoorlie.

Above: Kalgoorlie Town Hall.　　　　　　Below: York.

Below: York.

Below: Kalgoorlie.

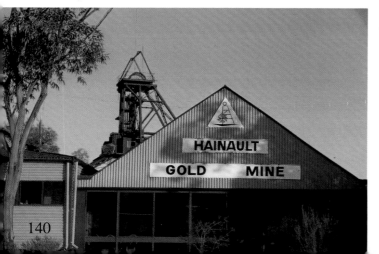

Above and below: Kalgoorlie.

Below: Kalgoorlie.

Above: Hamersley Range National Park.

Below: Kalbarri National Park.

Above and below: Ha

GIANT TERMITE MOUND

THIS MOUND WAS BUILT BY SPINIFEX TERMITES NASUTITERMES TRIODIAE
IT IS 3.7m HIGH AND POSSIBLY 100 YEARS OLD. BUT THE TERMITE
COLONY HAS NOW DIED OUT. THESE TERMITES EAT SPINIFEX SECTIONS
FOOD SUPPLIES IN THE THICK WALLED OUTER CHAMBERS.

PLEASE DO NOT DAMAGE OR CLIMB ON THE MOUND

ey Range National Park.

Below: Kalbarri National Park.